The Seasons of Life

*Ute Holm*
# The Seasons of Life

***Bibliographic Information from the German National Library***
The German National Library has registered this publication in the German National Bibliography; detailed bibliographic information can be found on the Internet at http://dnb.d-nb.de.

© 2014 Ute Holm
Cover design, typesetting, production and publishing house:
BoD – Books on Demand

ISBN 978-3-7357-4443-2

## Table of Contents

Preface   7

The Development   9

Trust Your Child   11

Genetic Structures   15

Mid-Life – A Time of Change   20

Health Before Beauty – Always   23

Remaining Professionally Active Until Old Age   26

The House and Advanced Age   30

Being Alone in Advanced Age   32

## *Preface*

This is a book about the individual stages of development we undergo in life, some of which we accept as normal, while other phases we may see as a threat. Many areas will be touched upon, and while they may not seem to make sense at first, they suddenly become clear when viewed as part of the larger picture. For example, we find ourselves asking: Why is it precisely my profession or partnership that is so chaotic? Why do I get sick so often? Why do so many things in my life go wrong?

There are always five pillars to our being. These can also be described as our inner values, which cannot be separated as they make up who we are and determine our entire life. If we are experiencing deficits on the human emotional level, our professional, financial and material levels will automatically fluctuate as well. These spiritual and physical levels form our base and control all of the levels mentioned above. Everything begins with the conception and then birth of a developed child.

From that point on, our lives will be characterized by the changes we go through as we grow old, changes that become apparent and make themselves known through difficult situations. These situations are the only way we recognize where work needs to be done. Everything that happens is natural and should be regarded in light of nature. External nature uses seasons to remind us we are subject to the laws of nature and how hard we try to work against natural processes. As humans, we like to suppress things and situations and we employ every tool we are given to forget, to mask the things we simply do not want to be true.

Beginning with the readily available cosmetic products or the other drugs that promise to heal all wounds and every wrinkle, anything that reminds us of the life behind us, the situations we have already mastered.

## *The Development*

People are not aware that we consist of living cells and that all of the cells and organs that compose our bodies work in harmony and in symbiosis with our brain, and it is exactly these connections that enable us to do what we do every day in the first place. Rejecting any part of our body is an insult to our entire body. Every development produces changes in our thinking, our figure, our skin. That is why development can be seen in every other area as well.

Every pregnancy leaves its traces, although these we accept gladly. We look forward to the new life, what will arise from it, how it will grow.

The basis for staying healthy is an intake of nutrients and newborns demand them at regular intervals, usually 3 to 4 times. The period of breastfeeding following birth is decisive. Every human has his or her own rhythm, which they need to follow. As a mother, one's focus turns to the newborn and finds peace at feeding time. Since daily routines, the parents' professional lives, etc. are often very stressful, children are often forced to adjust to changing situations. Feeding is delayed or parents simply skip a meal. Meals are considered a necessity to be taken care of on the side. The natural process and the corresponding sensation of being hungry are deactivated. "I don't want to get fat" is a common justification heard among young adults, who learn the behavior from their parents. Health issues naturally affect every area of our lives and make the transition to the next stage of development difficult. People distracted at mealtimes, whether through television, reading, or other activities, tend to eat in an uncontrolled manner, which generally leads to over eating and translates into weight gain and sluggishness, often resulting in the need for treatment.

## *Trust Your Child*

Your child was born healthy and has the big dream of discovering the world. Everyone welcomes the first attempts at walking or speaking. As a child continues to develop, helping hands are actively there to guide him or her. The child cannot do this or that alone, it is too dangerous. Later, the child cannot clean his or her own room, cannot finance something himself or herself, or cannot manage whatever the child happens to be faced with. Accompanying a child through all of the important everyday activities it will face and which will increase by the day, and teaching the child to take responsibility for him or herself and for others, gives the child the opportunity to prove him or herself, I can do it. The child's self-esteem grows and he or she is less afraid of new tasks he or she will face in school. The child learns to be proactive, to realize thoughts and ideas, which is very important, for example, when choosing a profession. Children for whom everything is done lack many key developmental processes, including the ability to make mistakes that allow them to readjust. Parents always want the best for their children, which is why they often tend to do too much. The result is that they end up making their children dependent. That is also how parents make themselves indispensable to their children. It is much better to allow children to engage in an independent adult life, in which they can stand on their own two feet and manage most of the things in their lives by themselves. Every healthy child has the natural aspiration to walk on their own, to independently answer the questions life presents and to make its own decisions. As a parent, one has to learn to let the child go and to make him or her responsible for his or her own, because it is the child's life and no longer the life of the parent. Healthy support can be provided by preparing a child for everything that lies ahead: "You can do it, keep up the good work." "Don't worry about it, I'll take care of it" doesn't help anyone. It also makes parents proud to have such a strong child, not to have to worry what will happen if the parent isn't there.

Young adults encouraged in this manner have goals and dreams they are willing to work for. Academic studies or the selection of a profession are no problem, because they already know what they want. The ambition they need has already been awakened and goals are quickly attained. Things always move forward and difficulties are quickly overcome. Their self-elected professional forms the basis for their life, for relationships and for establishing a family. A profession is especially important for women. It gives them a sense of security in life, particularly if a relationship happens to runs into trouble. Even if a woman has not been active in the profession for years, the simple fact of having learned one in the first place, of having a basis for further education and a determination to resume a profession, will guarantee she advances. It is very important to participate in the pulse of life, not to get stuck, not to give up when things get difficult. These learning processes give us back our value, which we may have lost somewhere along the long line of life. New goals bring movement into our lives. We remember who we are, what we are and what we are capable of. Equal partners treat one another better, accept one another as individuals who have something to say. The independence obtained through one's career does not mean the end of family. Self-secure people have a strong ability to trust others and often have good manners, which supports harmony. A career means security for every person, regardless of the phase of life they happen to be in. Major turning points in life give a career new meaning and are vital to life. A job is something too, but never provides enough security to cover our financial needs; however, a learned profession is always there when you need it. It can be rediscovered through advanced training and continues to give us new perspectives, a sense of approval and introduce us to new people, even as we grow old, so that nothing stands between us and a long, beautiful, active life. Active employment also means opening ourselves up to what life has to offer and doing so with self-discipline, actively and with good health. After all, we are always entitled to time off. With the right approach to life, doors will open, even as we grow older, we simply have to want it.

Those who retire too early, or let themselves be helped too much as they grow older, run the risk of giving up on themselves. The more we actually do for ourselves in life, pushing ourselves even as we grow older, the more accepted we will be, even among the young. We show our strengths, are taken seriously and create the freedom we need to start new projects. Those who have learned a lot in life always have the option of remaining active, which in turn, gives them financial freedom, allowing them to maintain what they have built up.

There are many ways to remain healthy, even when older, but the most important are honesty and a fast belief in oneself, once again, truly wanting it. Unfortunately, we are sometimes quick to embrace an illness, whether to get attention or because we consider it to simply come with age; however, we can also promote positive thinking, build ourselves up when life asks too much of us, because it is not always work that makes our lives hard. Rather, it is unclarified personal situations that we have not resolved.

## *Genetic Structures*

The female egg cell, which is known to be the largest cell, already contains certain genetic material, which, when combined with the sperm cell, the male genetic material, creates life. Development begins. This merging of genetic systems determines the rest of one's life, from birth until the end of life. It is like a program our path follows. It is also a package we each carry and which no one can carry for us. Everyone has to find a way. Some are plagued with addictions, others with guilt, illness or a constant shortage of money. Whatever it is, we carry it with us.

How can we deal with it? How can we know what sort of package we have?

The contents become clear fairly quickly, you simply have to look at a child's characteristics. How we treat young, impressionable people is very important and requires parents to be very sensitive. It often very challenging for parents to try to understand a child that cannot yet speak. To assume that responsibility as a parent is to place one's own needs aside. That means, making sure a child gets its meals and maintaining its sleep patterns, not continuously waking them up, etc. Basically, all of the simple things we do not want others doing to us either. This further means, that children are also influenced by how we treat ourselves. If we are not careful with ourselves, children will also fall by the so-called wayside. They then lack the values that should have shaped the rest of their lives. The more a parent can give a child, such as a sense of responsibility, knowledge or good manners, the more and easier it is for the child to develop. The values are already in place and no longer have to be figured out; one could almost say those values help shape the academic and professional paths. Which, in turn, determine the financial well-being, work ethic and many other aspects. However, this can only be achieved if the child is given the opportunity to discover himself or herself and his or her world. Meaning, that while we assist a child in many things, at some point we have to let go and allow the child to do them on his or her own. This tells them, "I know you are capable, so go ahead and do it!" regardless of the type of activity. Deciding to raise a child also means explaining why something has to be done. Doing everything for a child, along the lines of "let me just do it, it will be faster" or "he or she is still so little and can't manage", is a type of help that is actually no help at all. By doing so, you are also taking away the child's ability to show you what he or she is capable of. It is always the right time once the child indicates he or she wants to do it. Walking alone, helping clean up, etc. That is what I mean by sensitivity. Being aware of the child and what he or she wants, allowing the child to follow an idea. At the same time, there also needs to be a firm "no" for things that are dangerous, but this needs to be accompanied by an explanation of why.

To ensure children know their boundaries, it is also important to be constant. Yes is yes. And no is no. "Maybe" means nothing and a child begins plotting one parent against the other, and knows exactly what he or she can get from each one.

All of these small and major building blocks determine how a child will behave in a new environment, and children will be faced with new environments, whether daycare, school, college, university or apprenticeships, and later will also determine their willingness to work. The child's own sense of consequence can be seen here. If my child is determined, knows what he or she wants, knows early on what he or she wants to do when he or she grows up because such things are discussed at home, and does not change degrees half way through his or her studies, then everything is fine. The child will attack the rest of his or her life with the same determination. The parents have managed to turn the small child into a stable adult who will go through life strong and will accomplish anything her or she sets his or her mind to. Every parent's dream. Mistakes on this basic level lead to constant worries that can impact everyone's health. This is how dependencies are created and how addictions and hardships on many levels lead to discontent.

One's career is the most important foundation of a person's life, it nourishes and accompanies us throughout our entire life. Something has been created that we can fall back on.

It nourishes the spirit and this manifests itself in the form of inventiveness and the translation thereof. Having many interests leads to further goals, travels and a general willingness to embrace the world, as well as polite manners and honest business or business dealings. One thing is linked to another. That which we learned, grows and expands. It takes a good, positive person to see and understand his or her success. There is no space for sadness or depression. This person is in full bloom and enjoys life. He or she is standing in the sun. The stress of everyday life is no problem, nothing is too much, because that person knows where he or she stands and what he or she is capable of.

Among the haves and have nots, this person is among the former. Money can also be defined as profit:

> Success
> Reward
> Gratitude
> Money

Profit, in this case, being all of the good things that person learned growing up, the people he or she is surrounded by at work and who give him or her the chance for success, the reward, which is reflected by his or her bank account, and gratitude in the form of the recognition he or she receives for the major effort he or she has made, which again, is reflected in the recognition he or she receives from colleagues or the boss in the form of praise.

It is precisely during this, the prime of life, that one starts a family, and all of the values we learned are now passed on. We are the role models for our children.

If we become parents at too young an age, we ourselves lack the basis to provide sound support for our offspring. Everything we learn shapes us, it is saved in our cells. It is part of us and is what makes a person. For our children to have a better life than we did, we must begin with spiritual nourishment, which also tends to lead to a healthy macroscopic diet and not to anorexia.

Being firm and stable also means going your own way, not always being influenced by others, going along to get along or being dependent.

It is certainly not easy to find the right time to let go of one's child, but as hard as it may be, it must be done. Parents set the basis for this break by talking about it and it should be the young adult's career that provides a stable financial situation, allowing him or her to finance and master the new life situation.

This is a time of success, one in which a person develops, enters into their own partnerships and establishes themselves in everything they have built up.

## *Mid-Life – A Time of Change*

Thus, in the course of our lives, another phase materializes, one which we are not as willing to accept as the above-mentioned prime of our lives. It is the beginning of a period of significant cleansing and extraction, a time we consciously refer to as the "change". We perceive it consciously, as for many people it is associated with mood swings, discontent, a sense of unwell being or even illness. Our subconscious slowly begins to open the doors we had closed in the past, due to injuries we suffered from other people or our own dependencies, which we inflicted on others. The negative thoughts stored deep within us begin triggering physical pain to bring our attention to the fact that there is something we need to work on. It is important we take the time to ask why. Psychological discussions or feedback can potentially produce good results and should be taken advantage of. Every depression is a recovery phase and actually the best thing that can happen to a person. When handled properly, it will soon be water under the bridge. These are fully natural processes that are indicated by pain, because the body always gives us signs when something is not right. Take hunger for example. What happens? Our stomach growls. If we ignore that signal, the body reacts with circulation problems and nausea. If we still fail to react, our sugar levels will drop and we faint. Our organs all work in a close relationship to the brain, the central nervous system, which controls all of our physical reactions. This close relationship is also what allows the above-mentioned symptoms to manifest, allowing us to process them. If a person is then capable of forgiving themselves, others or situations, they will have achieved a great deal. Cleansed in this manner, they will be able to enjoy this time of maturity. Depending on the specific constellation, the mid-life phase can last up to 20 years. But, with the right mind-set and good company, it is a time that can be passed through well. Important during this phase is to recognize the changes and consequently permit them, let the past go. This may also include some rather significant life changes that are not as pleasant, which we do admit or allow as readily for fear we will no longer be as independent, perhaps because of our own personal financial situation. It is at this point, at the latest, that the profession we learned once again takes on importance. This is our personal foundation that we can build on. We do not forget what we have learned. The cells in our body, including our organs, never forget. It is one of nature's greatest gifts that we are capable of this cleansing and extraction, since nature – with its power to heal itself – is always able to help itself, and is always working to preserve itself. We are a large part of nature. Everything about us, every single cell we consist of, is alive and has earned the right to be treated well, to be accepted, to be thanked from time to time and not simply to take in one complaint after the other. We should accept our reflection and not simply correct, change our bodies. Thus, it is normal to accept the occasional wrinkle here or there as we age or a slightly fuller figure. We can only develop and progress by getting older. Part of this is the physical changes to our figure, as well as greater spiritual maturity. If we can accept the changes we are faced with throughout our lives, it is absolutely possible for us to live to a very old age, while remaining fit and healthy, giving ourselves the opportunity to rediscover life yet once again and to be accepted as a mature person by the world around us. One preventative health measure that we ourselves can take is to maintain the right, honest approach to life and to extract negative thoughts. We must do this ourselves as no one can think for us or master life for us nor does anyone know us or our situation better than we do. If we do not allow control to be taken from us as we age, if we manage to take care of our own needs and if we prevail in matters, then we can still stand in the middle of life, with our feet firmly on the ground: living situation, financial situation, etc. The self-healing processes always place a high demand on the body and it is not uncommon for them to become a permanent stress factor, producing a wide range of symptoms in the body. Thus, it is always a good idea to have preventative check-ups and see a doctor on a regular basis.

## *Health Before Beauty – Always*

Today's world places a special focus on going through life healthy and beautiful. Naturally, we would always prefer to have everything at once. When we are young, we never worry about smooth skin, since ours is firm, we have rosy cheeks and nary a wrinkle to be seen. That all changes relatively quickly as we age. Our lifestyles change, we begin to manipulate our bodies, follow diets to stop the first signs of changes in our figures. But they simply appear with age and, somehow, belong to our age, although they can be fairly well regulated through corresponding athletic measures. We spend too much time under the sun to combat the paleness incurred from poor nutrition or pathogens, such as nicotine or alcohol or other drugs. All of these things slip in unnoticed and leave our skin looking stressed, tired and dry. The first step is to become aware of how we are living, to make a permanent change and be consequent about enforcing those changes. We help our bodies with this purification, by being aware of what we eat and eating on a regular basis, by taking in enough liquids and exercising regularly. Although we should ask our physician about exercise, since not every type of sport will be equally beneficial, especially if we are already experiencing some health problems. Our skin is the largest excretion organ and immediately reacts to even the smallest changes. Changes affect the hydrolipidic film of our skin and we see dry or greasy skin, which can be corrected through cosmetic preparations. This process is not complete until we have successfully completed our inner cleansing process as well. In other words, it takes a while for this cleansing to become a permanent success that is also reflected on our skin. Cosmetic products can merely ease the way. Even the most effective products only improve our skin for a limited time. The actual reasons behind our skin problems always catch up with us, as nature is always stronger than anything we do to counteract it. And it is always up to us to decide which side we stand on, but we need to remember that anything we do that does not promote a healthy body, will catch up with us sooner or later. Regular visits to a beautician are always a good idea and not only are they relaxing, they can also provide us with information on the current state of our skin and which products might be good for us at the moment. Well-trained beauticians are generally more than happy to advise on the pros and cons when selecting which product from the wide variety of normal active ingredient cosmetics will be most effective for us, allowing us to use our own authority to make the right decision. Health, the corresponding radiance and beauty are all things we must work for. Our skin is a reflection of our soul, which cannot be concealed with decorative cosmetics. The healthier an organism is, the better we feel and the more positively we structure our lives. We also take aging and all of its demands in stride, nothing stands in the way of a long, active life, even in old age. All of these are things we realize internally, no one else can truly help us accomplish it. We ourselves are most familiar with our own situations and we are the only ones who can make a change when something is not right.

The new period in our life begins with restructuring and planning the new-found freedom in our lives, and it needs structure. We need hobbies, areas of interest, either ones we have always had or new ones we are discovering along the way. We have to activate these interests. They will involve new challenges, new people and tasks, which in a way complete the transition away from professional activity. They give us meaning, while giving us peace, allowing us to enjoy the years without pressure or stress. Undertaking new tasks will also provide us with a sense of satisfaction. Boredom does not stand a chance. Traveling when we are older is also wonderful and is to be highly recommended. Yet, if we are simply running away from ourselves or our life situation, we will never find peace. Active transitions begin with the question of how we want to live and what we should or must change to get there. Traveling is something we likely did even during our profession. Vacations were granted in due time and we probably took advantage of them. Those of us who accept our continued development, who are brave enough to move forward, live in harmony with nature as nature also makes every attempt to preserve itself. We are a living part of natural processes, processes we ourselves can undergo and complete if we so choose. The continuous transitions in our lives mean we exist parallel to nature, accompany nature in our shared seasons. Thus, it is only natural, that there are many things we accomplish in spring and summer, working actively to promote changes, while the fall and winter bring calm and the ability to see life through more relaxed eyes.

## *Remaining Professionally Active Until Old Age*

People who engage in an independent occupation up to old age undergo these highs and lows with ease, and with a proper approach toward what they are doing. The professional financial aspect in particular places high demands. Everything we do is directly related to the old genetic structures, which follow us right into our professional lives. Those who have never worked in the independent sector, most likely will not be very interested in doing so when they are older. If you allow yourself to sink into retirement, the aging process may set in relatively quickly. Allowing things to be done for you, even simple things, will cause you to become lethargic and it will not be long until another is granted authority over you. It is better to face life's challenges as long as we can, to assert ourselves wherever possible, to build up the strength to prove ourselves. Can I manage all that again? What do the people I interact with think of me? How credible am I now that I am older? Straighten out your bank accounts in a big way, especially if things are not as financially rosy as you would like. This can be managed by scaling back your demands significantly if necessary, keeping accounts within their limits, stretching out your liabilities, meaning, settling accounts step by step. Such steps show sound business sense, including talking openly with companies and upholding your agreements.

Companies that will probably suit your style will tend to be very accommodating. Companies that show resistance, should be avoided, this is an important step in the sorting process as well. It is the negative experiences that force us to make the changes that are long overdue. Naturally, business partners expect the same surety from you and give you a certain amount of freedom with your payments, they know you will pay. This allows you to go through certain lows without giving up. Because to give up is to lose.

There are also professional activities that can be performed with advancing age. Progress makes no exception here and simply means refocusing and doing something we have never done before. We reawaken intellectual realms and accomplish things that give us new strength, allowing us to share in the joy of life. We simply have to want it and do it. These activities will introduce us to like-minded people and even more interests will come into play. Those who bear the mind-set that they have already worked enough should rethink their position and consider how they wish to live, since work is the activity of doing something, being recognized and staying recognized, having a say, belonging. Simply remaining capable of action, capable of doing business, capable of employment.

Those who fail to push themselves in their youth will have many deficits on all key levels of life.

Pushing oneself intellectually also means spiritual and physical activity, which equate to feeling good about life, a sense of balance and health. Naturally, none of this replaces the need for preventative care with a physician, but self-healing in the sense of self-preservation is something active and makes us much more positive. Preventative care begins with a sensitivity and awareness of our own person, intentionally eating well, getting enough sleep, avoiding toxins in the form of nicotine and other drugs, drinking enough liquid. In other words, simply making sure the body feels good, making that morning glance in the mirror possible, and it is always worthwhile to give that reflection the recognition it deserves, with a compliment for example, "Hello. Good morning, you are looking good! You must be doing things right!" Behind that image is the person, who wants to be seen by others in that positive light as well. Appreciating ourselves will draw others to appreciate us as well. Our work will receive greater recognition or praise and suddenly work will not simply be work, but something we enjoy doing. It gives us a feeling of confirmation and the "I have to" becomes "I want to work".

If that which we do experiences success to boot, that is simply further confirmation that we are doing everything right. This increases our will to live. That is what we all want. A long, healthy life. However, we have to be willing to contribute and accept the changes we go through, they never stop. Unless, of course, we decide we no longer wish to grow and progress.

Everyone determines how they wish to live their own life. We live according to our needs and should not allow others to stop us. It is always about us, our own path in life, which is not always the same as everyone else's. What is good and right for one person, may not be suitable at all for another. This is where people go their separate ways. Sometimes we share a stretch of the road, then realize that the path is too rocky for the other. It is important to recognize this and to act accordingly, instead of blocking one another, as that only makes people unhappy and sick.

## *The House and Advanced Age*

For many older people it is difficult to change their living situation. Especially, if a few people are convinced they have to influence the older person. The house is too big, too expensive, too difficult to maintain, etc. The negative-minded people are basing their opinions on their own life and financial situation. It is important to follow one's own needs. Because often, it is not until we are older that we can actually stop and enjoy that which we worked so many years to acquire. Why, then, should we sacrifice comfort and space, especially when we are older? Here again, it is important to maintain our independence as long as possible. The cornerstone for this type of thinking and action is set by leading an active life, from youth until old age. It is a matter of self-worth and the quality of life we are accustomed to, which should be a particular priority in advanced age. Our biological age is irrelevant, as long as we do not feel old or inferior. Those who continue to take care of things themselves, who do not ask for help with everything, have the best chances of leading a comfortable, nice, rich life. To do so, it is important to see life's challenges as an opportunity to grow, not to get stuck. Instead – similar to the career phase of our lives – to actively participate in life. Intellectual activities should be in the foreground, such as shopping without a list, reading good books, exercising. Having many conversations and, when possible, going for a walk or a drive in your own car.

Anything is possible if we truly want it. What do you want?

It is true that finding the right approach to life often depends on familial circumstances. As a result, separations, illness or other worries can have a very negative impact on our ambition, our sense of "I want to", or may even make us sick ourselves. But even, or particularly, in these cases, it is important not to abandon our own path. We must face the situations and not let ourselves be beaten down. Because one thing is certain, life goes on, even if it does not always seem like it.

## *Being Alone in Advanced Age*

Many people complain about loneliness. Yet, only those who withdraw, who do not do something with their life, who ignore everything described above, who give in to their illness to get attention, end up lonely. This is not always a conscious decision. Rather, we are sometimes weakened by our life experiences, we sometimes give our past too much power over us, we resign, struggle with ourselves and our environment. These situations can assume sizable dimensions and it is not uncommon for there to be psychological consequences. We feel alone. It is usually one of life's turning points that cause us to behave in this manner. Life is a great balancing act. Thus, it is always important – no matter how hard life becomes – to place ourselves on the sunny side of life. Self-motivation makes it possible. The greatest hurdle can be mastered through our own powers of suggestion.

The brain takes in and reacts to what we give it and we live accordingly. If we tell it, "I'm not doing well, I have pain, worries, other cares", the body shows exactly that.

We can transform everything that happens into a positive, through our thoughts or the words we speak or by writing a letter to the situation in question. As a result, the act will turn out positively. Thus, it is in our own power to determine how we want to live and act. Self-worth determines how we live and we appear capable, solvent and employable, while receiving recognition and confirmation from others. Intellectual activity leads to physical activity. The more we process, by which I mean the cleansing of the old genetic structures, the healthier and more mobile we will be. The body produces signs for everything that bothers it through feelings of unwellness, sadness or pain. Those who pay close attention to themselves, can react quickly to their perceptions and turn negative energy into positive energy. This, in turn, allows them to do many things to remain or become healthy. That is what is meant by positive thinking. However, it is not enough to merely push special situations aside, they have to actually be dealt with. The body signalizes this process not only through heat waves or chills, but also through sadness, tears and joy. This act of cleansing is extremely hard work for the body. Thus, it is better not to diet when working through things, as you do not want to stress the body even more. It is completely normal to withdraw during such times, so as not to burden family and friends. Unfortunately, this is often seen as something negative and others tend to try to convince you to do things they see as being normal. Yet, it is better to decide for yourself, as certain activities may be too much for you in that moment and may cause you to feel worse than it really is, as you are now under a double burden. It is always a sign that those people are not able to put themselves in your position. They mean well, but are acting wrong. Once we have finished processing something, we can open ourselves back up to the community. Not only do we ourselves tend to change during these cleansing and extraction processes, but, as a result, we often change our life situation or professional situation, and thereby our group of friends as well. These processes can be concealed or delayed by taking medications, but never resolved. When you stop taking the medication, the situation returns in full force. Nature is always strong and through the process of cleansing and extracting, it gives us the opportunity to lead a healthy, beautiful and – if you will – a rich life, even in advanced age. We make a new group of friends.

The things that are good for us win though, harmony establishes itself and everything else falls by the wayside. If we are capable of consciously experiencing this time of cleansing and extraction, if we can accept it as a normal process, with all of its highs and lows, as the changes in life we go through from the time we are conceived. Everyone faces them at different ages and in their own specific way. It is the package that everyone carries with them and must process on their own. This also explains why children and young people have to suffer through fluctuations. When and at what age something has to be processed is decided by nature. It opens the subconscious, the site where the old genetic structures are stored. Everything that is released corresponds to our own personality and, thus, we should not be afraid of these processes; however, it is also good to get professional help when the demands become too great and we are no longer able to see clearly. Physicians and psychologists are always willing to help. The last major cleansing and extraction we face, which we refer to as mid-life or change, is also coupled with the greatest physical symptoms and external signs of aging. Our hair begins to turn gray or thin, the first wrinkles appear, our figure begins to fill out, we gain weight. All of this combined with any pain we may be experiencing, usually from past injuries, whether verbal or physical, all begins to make itself known. When these factors combine, we get a certain feeling of dissatisfaction and begin to prepare for the "big change", which can take many years and reminds us of nature, that which we have grown from. The living cells that now demand our attention, beg for recognition and praise, and do not want to be scorned. Those who accept every stage of their life, the highs and lows, can move on, strengthened and motivated. They can take in the every-changing seasons, in all of their glorious and brightest colors.

*

This book is a summary of years of practical experience dealing with people I have trained or have accompanied as a mentor. These are people of various ages, in various life situations, who built up their personality, thereby finding the way to independence. If we allow the younger generation to take authority over our lives too early on, by allowing ourselves to be assisted in areas where we simply fail to take responsibility, we are giving up. We will feel confined, somehow mistreated, and unhappy. Our only choice is to go it alone, not to give up control over our own matters, to make our own decisions and be responsible for them. To be the masters of our lives. Every person has their own goals and their own path to follow to reach the door to success.